WASHINGTON ON COURAGE

WASHINGTON ON COURAGE

George Washington's Formula for Courageous Living

GEORGE WASHINGTON

Skyhorse Publishing

Skyhorse Publishing books may be purchased in bulk
at special discounts for sales promotion, corporate
gifts, fund-raising, or educational purposes. Special
editions can also be created to specifications. For
details, contact the Special Sales Department, Skyhorse
Publishing, 307 West 36th Street, 11th Floor, New York,
NY 10018 or info@skyhorsepublishing.com.

www.skyhorsepublishing.com

10 9 8 7 6 5 4 3 2 1

Library of Congress Cataloging-in-Publication Data is
available on file.

ISBN: 978-1-5107-5580-2

Printed in the United States of America

CONTENTS

PART 1:

1775, July–December.   1

PART 2:

1776, January–February   45

PART 3:

1777, July–December.   67

PART 4:

1778, February–July   109

The time is now near at hand which must probably determine whether Americans are to be freemen or slaves; whether they are to have any property they can call their own; whether their houses and farms are to be pillaged and destroyed, and themselves consigned to a state of wretchedness from which no human efforts will deliver them. The fate of unborn millions will now depend, under God, on the courage and conduct of this army. Our cruel and unrelenting enemy leaves us only the choice of brave resistance, or the most abject submission. We have, therefore, to resolve to conquer or die.

GEORGE WASHINGTON,
address to the Continental Army before the
battle of Long Island, Aug. 27, 1776

To be prepared for War is one of the most effectual means of preserving peace.

GEORGE WASHINGTON,
first annual address to Congress,
Jan. 8, 1790

PART 1:

1775

July–December

Every post is honorable in which a man can serve his country.

Answer to an Address of the Provincial Congress of Massachusetts[1], 4 July, 1775

Gentlemen,

Your kind congratulations on my appointment and arrival, demand my warmest acknowledgments, and will ever be retained in grateful remembrance.

In exchanging the enjoyments of domestic life for the duties of my present honorable but arduous station, I only emulate the virtue and public spirit of the whole province of Massachusetts Bay, which, with a firmness,

---

[1] General Washington arrived in Cambridge on the 2d of July, and took command of the army on the 3d. The Massachusetts Congress were at this time convened at Watertown, three miles from Cambridge, and on his arrival they honored him with a congratulatory address.

and patriotism without example in modem history, has sacrificed all the comforts of social and political life, in support of the rights of mankind, and the welfare of our common country. My highest ambition is to be the happy instrument of vindicating those rights, and to see this devoted province again restored to peace, liberty, and safety.

The short space of time, which has elapsed since my arrival, does not permit me to decide upon the state of the army. The course of human affairs forbids an expectation, that troops formed under such circumstances should at once possess the order, regularity, and discipline of veterans. Whatever deficiencies there may be, will, I doubt not, soon be made up by the activity and zeal of the officers, and the docility and obedience of the men. These qualities, united with their native bravery and spirit, will afford a happy presage of success, and put a final period to those distresses, which now over-whelm this once happy country.

I most sincerely thank you, Gentlemen, for your declarations of readiness at all times to assist me in the discharge of the duties of my station. They are so complicated and extended, that I shall need the assistance of every good man, and lover of his country. I therefore repose the utmost confidence in your aid. In return for your affectionate wishes to myself, permit me to say, that I earnestly implore that divine Being, in whose hands are all human events, to make you and your constituents as distinguished in private and public happiness, as you have been by ministerial oppression, and by private and public distress.

To the President of Congress, Camp at Cambridge, 10 July, 1775

Sir,

I arrived safe at this place on the 3d instant, after a journey attended with a good deal of fatigue, and retarded by necessary attentions to the successive civilities, which accompanied me in my whole route.

Upon my arrival, I immediately visited the several posts occupied by our troops; and, as soon as the weather permitted, reconnoitered those of the enemy. I found the latter strongly intrenching on Bunker's Hill, about a mile from Charlestown, and advanced about half a mile from the place of the late action, with their sentries extended about one hundred and fifty yards on this side of the narrowest part of the neck leading from this place to Charlestown. Three floating batteries lie in Mystic River near their camp, and one twenty-gun ship below the ferry-place between Boston and Charlestown. They have also a battery on Cops Hill, on the Boston side, which much annoyed our troops in the late attack. Upon Roxbury Neck, they are also deeply intrenched and strongly fortified. Their advanced guards, till last Saturday, occupied Brown's houses, about a mile from Roxbury meeting-house, and twenty rods from their lines; but, at that time, a party from General Thomas's camp surprised the guard, drove them in, and burned the houses. The bulk of their army, commanded by General Howe, lies on Bunker's Hill, and the remainder on Roxbury Neck, except the light-horse, and a few men in the town of Boston.

On our side, we have thrown up intrenchments on Winter and Prospect Hills, the enemy's camp in full view, at

the distance of little more than a mile.
Such intermediate points as would admit a
landing, I have since my arrival taken care
to strengthen, down to Sewall's farm, where
a strong intrenchment has been thrown up.
At Roxbury, General Thomas has thrown
up a strong work on the hill, about two
hundred yards above the meeting-house;
which, with the brokenness of the ground,
and a great number of rocks, has made
that pass very secure. The troops raised
in New Hampshire, with a regiment from
Rhode Island, occupy Winter Hill; a part
of those from Connecticut, under General
Putnam, are on Prospect Hill. The troops in
this town are entirely of the Massachusetts;
the remainder of the Rhode Island men are
at Sewall's farm. Two regiments of Connecticut, and nine of the Massachusetts, are at
Roxbury. The residue of the army, to the
number of about seven hundred, are posted

in several small towns along the coast, to prevent the depredations of the enemy.

Upon the whole, I think myself authorized to say, that, considering the great extent of line and the nature of the ground, we are as well secured, as could be expected in so short a time, and with the disadvantages we labor under. These consist in a want of engineers to construct proper works and direct the men, a want of tools, and a sufficient number of men to man the works in case of an attack. You will observe, by the proceedings of the council of war, which I have the honor to enclose, that it is our unanimous opinion, to hold and defend these works as long as possible. The discouragement it would give the men, and its contrary effects on the ministerial troops, thus to abandon our encampment in their face, formed with so much labor and expense, added to the certain destruction of a considerable and valuable extent of country, and our uncertainty of finding a place in all respects so capable of making a stand, are leading reasons for this determination. At the same time we are very sensible of the difficulties, which attend the defence of lines of so great extent, and the dangers, which may ensue from such a division of the army.[2]

---

[2] The first council of war was held at head-quarters on the 9th of July, attended by the major-generals and the brigadiers. The council decided, that, from the best information, the number of the enemy's forces in Boston should be estimated at eleven thousand five hundred men. On the question whether it was expedient to defend the posts now occupied, or retire further into the country, it was unanimously determined to defend the posts. It was also agreed, that twenty-two thousand men at least were necessary to act against the supposed force of the enemy, and that measures ought to be immediately taken to increase the army by recruits. It was further agreed, that, if the troops should be attacked, and routed by the enemy, the place of rendezvous should be Wales's Hill, in the rear of the Roxbury lines.

My earnest wish to comply with the instructions of the Congress, in making an early and complete return of the state of the army, has led to an involuntary delay of addressing you; which has given me much concern. Having given orders for that purpose immediately on my arrival, and not then so well apprised of the imperfect obedience, which had been paid to those of the like nature from General Ward, I was led from day to day to expect they would come in, and therefore detained the messenger. They are not now so complete as I could wish; but much allowance is to be made for inexperience in forms, and a liberty which had been taken (not given) on this subject. These reasons, I flatter myself, will no longer exist; and, of consequence, more regularity and exactness will in future prevail. This, with a necessary attention to the lines, the movements of the ministerial troops, and our immediate security, must be my apology, which I beg you to lay before Congress with the utmost duty and respect.

We labor under great disadvantages for want of tents; for, though they have been helped out by a collection of sails from the seaport towns, the number is far short of our necessities. The colleges and houses of this town are necessarily occupied by the troops; which affords another reason for keeping our present station. But I most sincerely wish the whole army was properly provided to take the field, as I am well assured, that, besides greater expedition and activity in case of alarm, it would highly conduce to health and discipline. As materials are not to be had here, I would beg leave to recommend the procuring of a farther supply from Philadelphia, as soon as possible.

I should be extremely deficient in gratitude, as well as justice, if I did not take the first opportunity to acknowledge the readiness and attention, which the Provincial Congress and different committees have shown, to make every thing as convenient and agreeable as possible. [3] But there is a vital and inherent principle of delay incompatible with military service, in transacting business through such numerous and different channels. I esteem it, therefore, my duty to repre-

---

[3] Before General Washington left Philadelphia, he requested the Massachusetts delegates in Congress to recommend to him such bodies of men, and individuals, as he might apply to with confidence in that colony. They answered him in writing, and referred him particularly to the Committee on the State of the Province, the Committee of Safety, and the Committee of Supplies. They moreover enumerated the following gentlemen, as worthy and trusty friends of the cause, on whose judgment and fidelity he might rely, namely, Bowdoin, Sever, Dexter, Greenleaf, Pitts, Otis, of the late council; John Winthrop; Joseph Hawley, of Northampton; James Warren, of Plymouth; Colonel Palmer, of Braintree; Colonel Orne and Elbridge Gerry, of Marblehead; Dr. Warren, Dr. Church, John Pitts, Dr. Chauncy, Dr. Cooper, of Boston; Dr. Langdon, President of Harvard College; and Colonel Foster, of Brookfiled.— *MS. Letter, June 22d.*

sent the inconvenience, which must unavoidably ensue from a dependence on a number of persons for supplies; and submit it to the consideration of Congress, whether the public service will not be best promoted by appointing a commissary-general for these purposes. We have a striking instance of the preference of such a mode, in the establishment of Connecticut, as their troops are extremely well provided under the direction of Mr. Trumbull, and he has at different times assisted others with various articles. Should my sentiments happily coincide with those of your Honors on this subject, I beg leave to recommend Mr. Trumbull as a very proper person for this department. In the arrangement of troops collected under such circumstances, and upon the spur of immediate necessity, several appointments have been omitted, which appear to be indispensably necessary for the good government of the army, particularly a quartermaster-general, a commissary of musters, and a commissary of artillery. These I must particularly recommend to the notice and provision of the Congress. [4]

I find myself already much embarrassed, for want of a military chest. These embarrassments will increase every day. I must therefore most earnestly request, that money may be forwarded as soon as possible. The want of this most necessary article, will, I fear, produce great inconveniences, if not prevented by an early attention. I find the army in general, and the troops raised in Massachusetts in particular, very deficient in necessary clothing. Upon inquiry, there appears no probability of obtaining any supplies in this quarter; and, on the best consideration of this matter I am able to form, I am of opinion that a number of hunting-shirts, not less than ten thousand,

---

[4] When this application was considered by Congress, the appointment of these officers was left to the Commander-in-chief.

would in a great degree remove this difficulty, in the cheapest and quickest manner. I know nothing, in a speculative view, more trivial, yet which, if put in practice, would have a happier tendency to unite the men, and abolish those provincial distinctions, that lead to jealousy and dissatisfaction.

In a former part of this letter, I mentioned the want of engineers. I can hardly express the disappointment I have experienced on this subject, the skill of those we have being very imperfect, and confined to the mere manual exercise of cannon; whereas the war in which we are engaged requires a knowledge, comprehending the duties of the field, and fortification. If any persons thus qualified are to be found in the southern colonies, it would be of great public service to forward them with all expedition.

Upon the article of ammunition, I must reecho the former complaints on this subject. We are so exceedingly destitute, that our artillery will be of little use, without a supply both large and seasonable. What we have must be reserved for the small arms, and that managed with the utmost frugality.

I am very sorry to observe, that the appointment of general officers, in the provinces of Massachusetts and Connecticut, has not corresponded with the wishes and judgment of either the civil or military. The great dissatisfaction expressed on this subject, and the apparent danger of throwing the whole army into the utmost disorder, together with the strong representations made by the Provincial Congress, have induced me to retain the commissions in my hands until the pleasure of the Continental Congress should be further known, except General Putnam's, which was given the day I came to the camp, and before I was apprized of these disgusts. In such a step, I must beg the Congress will do me the justice to believe, that I have been actuated solely by a regard to the public good.

I have not, nor could I have, any private attachments; every gentleman in appointment was a stranger to me, but from character; I must, therefore, rely upon the candor and indulgence of Congress, for their most favorable construction of my conduct in this particular. General Spencer's disgust was so great at General Putnam's promotion, that he left the army without visiting me, or making known his intention in any respect.

General Pomroy had also retired before my arrival, occasioned, as it is said, by some disappointment from the Provincial Congress. General Thomas is much esteemed, and most earnestly desired to continue in the service; and, as far as my opportunities have enabled me to judge, I must join in the general opinion, that he is an able, good officer; and his resignation would be a public loss. The postponing of him to Pomroy and Heath, whom he has commanded, would make his continuance very difficult, and probably operate on his mind, as the like circumstance did on that of Spencer. [5]

---

[5] Eight brigadier-generals for the Continental army were chosen by Congress on the 22d of June, in the following order: Seth Pomroy, of Massachusetts; Richard Montgomery, of New York; David Wooster, of Connecticut; William Heath, of Massachusetts; Joseph Spencer, of Connecticut; John Thomas, of Massachusetts; John Sullivan, of New Hampshire; Nathanael Greene, of Rhode Island. The commissions for these officers had been brought to camp by General Washington. He found great uneasiness prevailing, as to the comparative rank conferred by these appointments. The difficulties were in some degree removed by Pomroy's declining to serve, and by Spencer's consenting to take rank after Putnam. By this arrangement Thomas was made the first brigadier-general.—*Journal of Congress, July 19th* Pomroy behaved with great courage at the battle of Bunker's Hill, and although he declined joining the Continental army, yet he headed the militia of his neighbourhood, who marched to the Hudson River, when New Jersey was overrun by the enemy. He never returned from that expedition. He died at Peekskill in New York.—Swett's *History of Bunker-Hill Battle,* 2d ed. pp. 8, 53.

The state of the army you will find ascertained with tolerable precision in the returns, which accompany this letter. Upon finding the number of men to fall so far short of the establishment, and below all expectation, I immediately called a council of the general officers, whose opinion, as to the mode of filling up the regiments, and providing for the present exigency, I have the honor of enclosing, together with the best judgment we are able to form of the ministerial troops. From the number of boys, deserters, and negroes, that have been enlisted in the troops of this province, I entertain some doubts whether the number required can be raised here; and all the general officers agree, that no dependence can be put on the militia, for a continuance in camp, or regularity and discipline during the short time they may stay. This unhappy and devoted province has been so long in a state of anarchy, and the yoke of ministerial oppression has been laid so heavily on it, that great allowances are to be made for troops raised under such circumstances. The deficiency of numbers, discipline, and stores, can only lead to this conclusion, that their spirit has exceeded their strength. But, at the same time, I would humbly submit to the consideration of Congress the propriety of making some further provision of men from the other colonies. If these regiments should be completed to their establishment, the dismission of those unfit for duty, on account of their age and character, would occasion a considerable reduction; and, at all events, they have been enlisted upon such terms, that they may be disbanded when other troops arrive. But should my apprehensions be realized, and the regiments here not be filled up, the public cause would suffer by an absolute dependence upon so doubtful an event, unless some provision is made against such a disappointment.

It requires no military skill to judge of the difficulty of introducing proper discipline and subordination into an army, while we have the enemy in view, and are in daily expectation of an attack; but it is of so much importance, that every effort will be made to this end, which time and circumstances will admit. In the mean time, I have a sincere pleasure in observing, that there are materials for a good army, a great number of able-bodied men, active, zealous in the cause, and of unquestionable courage.

I am now, Sir, to acknowledge the receipt of your favor of the 28th of June, enclosing the resolutions of Congress of the 27th, and a copy of a letter from the Committee of Albany; to all which I shall pay due attention.

Generals Gates and Sullivan have both arrived in good health.

My best abilities are at all times devoted to the service of my country; but I feel the weight, importance, and variety of my present duties too sensibly, not to wish a more immediate and frequent communication with the Congress. I fear it may often happen, in the course of our present operations, that I shall need that assistance and direction from them, which time and distance will not allow me to receive.

Since writing the above, I have also to acknowledge your favor of the 4th instant by Fessenden, and the receipt of the commissions and articles of war. Among the other returns, I have also sent one of our killed, wounded, and missing, in the late action;[6]

---

[6] At Bunker's Hill, on the 17th of June. According to a return published by the Provincial Congress of Massachusetts, the loss was one hundred and forty-five killed and missing, and three hundred and four wounded. About thirty of the first number were wounded and taken prisoner. By General Gage's official return, the killed and missing of the British were two hundred and twenty-six,

but have been able to procure no certain account of the loss of the ministerial troops. My best intelligence fixes it at about five hundred killed and six or seven hundred wounded; but it is no more than conjecture, the utmost pains being taken on their side to conceal their loss.

Having ordered the commanding officer to give me the earliest intelligence of every motion of the enemy by land or water, discernible from the heights of his camp, I this instant, as I was closing my letter, received the enclosed from the brigade-major. The design of this maneuver I know not; perhaps it may be to make a descent somewhere along the coast; it may be for New York; or it may be practised as a deception on us. I thought it not improper however to mention

and the wounded eight hundred and twenty-eight, in all one thousand and fifty four. –*Almon's Rememberancer*, Vol. I. pp. 99, 179.

the matter to you; I have done the same to the commanding officer at New-York; and I shall let it be known to the Committee of Safety here, so that intelligence may be communicated, as they shall think best, along the sea-coast of this government. I have the honor to be, &c.

To Jonathan Trumbull, Governor of Connecticut, Cambridge, 18 July, 1775

Sir,

Allow me to return you my sincere thanks, for the kind wishes and favorable sentiments expressed in yours of the 13th instant. As the cause of our common country calls us both to an active and dangerous duty, I trust that Divine Providence, which wisely orders the affairs of men, will enable us to discharge it with fidelity and success. The uncorrupted choice of a brave and free people has raised you to deserved eminence. That the blessings of health, and the still greater blessing of long continuing to govern such a people, may be yours, is the sincere wish of, Sir, your, &c. [7]

---

[7] Governor Trumbull was one of the firmest patriots and best men that his country has produced. He was at this time sixty-five years old, having been born in the year 1710, yet no man engaged with more zeal and activity

in the common cause. So true was he to the principles of liberty, and such was the confidence of his fellow citizens in his talents and integrity, that, although first appointed Governor in 1769, several years before the breaking out of the war, he was constantly chosen with great unanimity to the same station till the end of the revolution, when, at the age of seventy-three, he declined a further election. His services were of very great importance throughout the whole war, not only in regulating the civil affairs of Connecticut, but in keeping alive a military ardor among the people, and thus promoting efficiency and promptness of action in the forces contributed from time to time by that state. General Washington relied on him as one of his main pillars of support. The following extracts from Governor Trumbull's letter, to which the above is an answer, will show something of the spirit prevailing at that day, as well as the religious cast of the writer's mind;

"Suffer me to join in congratulating you, on your appointment to be General and Commander-in-chief of the troops raised or to be raised for the defence of American liberty. Men, who have tasted of freedom, and who have felt their personal rights, are not easily taught to bear with encroachments on either, or brought to submit to oppression. Virtue ought always to be made the object of government; justice is firm and permanent.

"His Majesty's ministers have artfully induced the Parliament to join in their measures, to prosecute the dangerous and increasing difference between Great Britain and these colonies with rigor and military force; whereby the latter are driven to an absolute necessity to defend their rights and properties, by raising forces

To Governor Cooke, of Rhode Island, Camp at Cambridge, 4 August, 1775

Sir,

I was yesterday favored with yours of the 31st of July. We have yet no certain accounts of the fleet, which sailed out of Boston on the 25th; but if our conjectures and information are just, we may expect to hear of it every hour.

---

for their security. The honorable Congress have, with one united voice, appointed you to the high station you possess. The Supreme Director of all events has caused a wonderful union of hearts and counsels to subsist amongst us. Now, therefore, be strong and very courageous. May the God of the armies of Israel shower down the blessings of his divine providence on you, give you wisdom and fortitude, cover your head in the day of battle and danger, add success, convince our enemies of their mistaken measures, and that all their attempts to deprive these colonies of their inestimable constitutional rights and liberties are injurious and vain."

I am now, Sir, in strict confidence, to acquaint you, that our necessities in the articles of powder and lead are so great, as to require an immediate supply. I must earnestly entreat, that you will fall upon some measure to forward every pound of each in your colony, that can possibly be spared. It is not within the propriety or safety of such a correspondence to say what I might on this subject. It is sufficient, that the case calls loudly for the most strenuous exertions of every friend of his country, and does not admit of the least delay. No quantity, however small, is beneath notice, and, should any arrive, I beg it may be forwarded as soon as possible.

But a supply of this kind is so precarious, not only from the danger of the enemy, but the opportunity of purchasing, that I have revolved in my mind every other possible chance, and listened to every proposition on the subject, which could give the smallest hope. Among others, I have had one mentioned, which has some weight with me, as well as the general officers to whom I have proposed it. A Mr. Harris has lately come from Bermuda, where there is a very considerable magazine of powder in a remote part of the island; and the inhabitants are well disposed not only to our cause in general, but to assist in this enterprise in particular. We understand there are two armed vessels in your province, commanded by men of known activity and spirit; one of which, it is proposed to despatch on this errand with such assistance as may be requisite. Harris is to go along, as the conductor of the enterprise, that we may avail ourselves of his knowledge of the island; but without any command. I am very sensible, that at first view the project may appear hazardous; and its success must depend on the concurrence of many circumstances; but we are in a situation, which requires us to run all risks. No danger is to be considered, when put in competition with the magnitude of the cause, and the absolute necessity we are under of increasing our stock. Enterprises, which appear chimerical, often prove successful from that very circumstance. Common sense and prudence will suggest vigilance and care, where the danger is plain and obvious; but, where little danger is apprehended, the more the enemy will be unprepared, and consequently there is the fairest prospect of success.

Mr. Brown has been mentioned to me as a very proper person to be consulted upon this occasion. You will judge of the propriety of communicating it to him in part or the whole, and as soon as possible favor me with your sentiments, and the steps you may have taken to forward it. If no immediate and safe opportunity offers, you will please to do it by express. Should it be inconvenient to part with one of the armed vessels, perhaps some other might be fitted out, or you could devise some other mode of executing this plan; so that, in case of a disappointment, the vessel might proceed to some other island to purchase.

We have had no transactions in either camp since my last, but what are in the public papers, and related with tolerable accuracy. The enemy still continue to strengthen their lines, and, we have reason to believe, intend to bombard ours, with the hope of forcing us out of them. Our poverty in ammunition prevents our making a suitable return.

Since writing the above, Colonel Porter has undertaken to assist in the matter, or to provide some suitable person to accompany Harris to you, who will communicate all the circumstances. I am, &c.

To Colonel Benedict Arnold, Camp at Cambridge, 14 September, 1775

Sir,

You are entrusted with a command of the utmost consequence to the interest and liberties of America. Upon your conduct and courage, and that of the officers and soldiers detached on this expedition, not only the success of the present enterprise, and your own honor, but the safety and welfare of the whole continent may depend. I charge you, therefore, and the officers and soldiers under your command, as you value your own safety and honor, and the favor and esteem of your country, that you consider yourselves, as marching not through the country of an enemy, but of our friends and brethren, for such the inhabitants of Canada, and the Indian nations, have approved themselves in this unhappy contest between Great Britain and America; and that you check, by every motive of duty and fear of punishment, every attempt to plunder or insult the inhabitants of Canada. Should any American soldier be so base and infamous as to injure any Canadian or Indian, in his person or property, I do most earnestly enjoin you to bring him to such severe and exemplary punishment, as the enormity of the crime may require. Should it extend to death itself, it will not be disproportioned to its guilt, at such a time and in such a cause.

But I hope and trust, that the brave men, who have voluntarily engaged in this expedition, will be governed by far different views; and that order, discipline, and regularity of behaviour, will be as conspicuous as their valor. I also give it in charge to you to avoid all disrespect of the religion of the country, and its ceremonies.

Prudence, policy, and a true Christian spirit, will lead us to look with compassion upon their errors without insulting them. While we are contending for our own liberty, we should be very cautious not to violate the rights of conscience in others, ever considering that God alone is the judge of the hearts of men, and to him only in this case they are answerable.

Upon the whole, Sir, I beg you to inculcate upon the officers and soldiers the necessity of preserving the strictest order during the march through Canada; to represent to them the shame, disgrace, and ruin to themselves and their country, if they should by their conduct turn the hearts of our brethren in Canada against us; and, on the other hand, the honors and rewards, which await them, if by their prudence and good behaviour they conciliate the affections of the Canadians and Indians to the great interests of

America, and convert those favorable dispositions they have shown into a lasting union and affection: Thus wishing you, and the officers and soldiers under your command, all honor, safety, and success, I remain, Sir, your most obedient humble servant.

To Governor Trumbull, Cambridge, 15 December, 1775

Sir,

Your favors of the 7th and 9th instant I received, and was much pleased to hear of the zeal of the people of Connecticut, and the readiness of the inhabitants of the several towns to march to this camp, upon their being acquainted with the behaviour and desertion of their troops. I have nothing to suggest for the consideration of your Assembly. I am confident they will not be wanting in their exertions for supporting the just and constitutional rights of the colonies.

Enclosed I send you a list of the officers and companies under the new establishment, with the number of the men enlisted; the returns only came in to-day, or I would have transmitted it before.

Having heard that it is doubtful whether the Reverend Mr. Leonard, from your colony, will have it in his power to continue here as a Chaplain, I cannot but express some concern, as I think his departure will be a loss. His general conduct has been exemplary and praiseworthy; in discharging the duties of his office, active and industrious; he has discovered himself a warm and steady friend to his country, and taken great pains to animate the soldiers, and impress them with a knowledge of the important rights we are contending for. Upon the late desertion of the troops, he gave a sensible and judicious discourse, holding forth the necessity of courage and bravery, and at the same time of obedience and subordination to those in command.

In justice to the merits of this gentleman, I thought it only right to give you this testimonial of my opinion of him, and to mention him to you, as a person worthy of your esteem and that of the public. I am, Sir, &c.

To Major-General Schuyler, Cambridge,
24 December, 1775

Dear Sir,

Your favor of the 15th instant came
yesterday to hand, with copies and extracts
of your late letters to Congress. I have with
great attention perused them. I am very sorry
to find by several paragraphs, that both you
and General Montgomery incline to quit the
service. Let me ask you, Sir, when is the time
for brave men to exert themselves in the cause
of liberty and their country, if this is not?
Should any difficulties, that they may have
to encounter at this important crisis, deter
them? God knows, there is not a difficulty,
that you both very justly complain of, which
I have not in an eminent degree experienced,
that I am not every day experiencing; but we
must bear up against them, and make the best
of mankind as they are, since we cannot have

them as we wish. Let me, therefore, conjure you and Mr. Montgomery to lay aside such thoughts, thoughts injurious to yourselves, and extremely so to your country, which calls aloud for gentlemen of your abilities.

You mention in your letter to Congress of the 20th ultimo, that the clothing was to remain at Albany, as General Montgomery would provide the troops in Canada. I wish they could be spared for this army, for we cannot get clothing for half of our troops. Let me hear from you on this subject as soon as possible.

The proofs you have of the ministry's intention to engage the savages against us are incontrovertible. We have other confirmations of it, by several despatches from John Stuart, the superintendent for the southern district, which luckily fell into my hands, being found on board a sloop, sent by Lord

Dunmore, bound to Boston. She was taken by one of our armed vessels. These, with many letters of consequence from his Lordship, I have lately sent to the Congress.

I hope soon to hear, that Colonel Knox has made good progress in forwarding the artillery.[8] It is much wanted for the works

---

[8] Colonel Knox had many obstacles to contend against in executing his charge, on account of the lateness of the season, and badness of the roads. By extraordinary energy and perseverance, however, which were marked traits of his character, he overcame them all, and effected his purpose. He wrote as follows to General Washington, from the head of Lake George, on the 17th of December.

"I returned from Ticonderoga to this place on the 15th instant, and brought with me the cannon, it having taken nearly the time I conjectured it would to transport them hither. It is not easy to conceive the difficulties we have had in getting them over the Lake, owing to the advanced season of the year and contrary winds. Three days ago, it was very uncertain whether we could get them over until next spring, but now, please God, they shall go. I have made forty-two exceedingly strong sleds, and have provided eighty yoke or oxen to drag them as we have lately thrown up. I have written a letter, of the 18th instant, to General Howe respecting Mr. Allen, of which and the answer you have copies enclosed. I am, with great regard, Sir, yours, &c.

far as Springfield, where I shall get fresh cattle to take them to camp."

PART 2:

1776

January–February

Let us therefore animate and encourage each other, and show the whole world that a Freeman, contending for liberty on his own ground, is superior to any slavish mercenary on earth.

To Colonel Benedict Arnold, Cambridge, 27 January, 1776

Dear Sir,

On the 17th instant I received the melancholy account of the unfortunate attack on the city of Quebec, attended with the fall of General Montgomery and other brave officers and men, and of your being wounded. This unhappy affair affects me in a very sensible manner, and I sincerely condole with you upon the occasion; but, in the midst of distress, I am happy to find, that suitable honors were paid to the remains of Mr. Montgomery; and that our officers and soldiers, who have fallen into their hands, were treated with kindness and humanity. [9]

---

[9] During the night of the attack on Quebec there was a tempestuous snow-storm. The bodies of the persons slain under the cliff of Cape Diamond were not discovered till morning, when they were found nearly enveloped in snow. They were taken into the city on a sled. Three of them were known to be officers, and from the initials R. M. written in a fur cap, picked up at the place of the bloody catastrophe, it was conjectured to have belonged to General Montgomery. His features were disfigured by a wound, which he had received in the lower part of the head and neck. At length a woman and a boy were brought, who had lately come into the city from the American camp, and who had often seen the principal officers. They identified the bodies of Montgomery, Captain McPherson, Captain Cheesman, and an orderly sergeant.

Mr. Cramahe, an officer in the British army, and for a time lieutenant-governor of Canada, had served in the last war with Montgomery, and entertained for him a warm personal attachment. He asked permission of General Carleton to bury his friend with marks of honor and respect. This was granted in part, and a coffin lined and covered with black was provided. But the Governor did not consent to the reading of the funeral service, probably not deeming this indulgence conformable to military rules. But when the time of burial approached, Mr. Cramahe invited a clergyman to be present, who read the service privately ad unmolested. The other

Having received no intelligence later than the copy of your letter of the 2d to General Wooster, I would fain hope, that you are not in a worse situation than you then were; though, I confess, I have greatly feared, that those misfortunes would be succeeded by others, on account of your unhappy condition, and the dispirited state of the officers and men. If they have not, I trust that when you are joined by three regiments now raising in this and the governments of Connecticut and New Hampshire, and two others ordered by the Congress from Pennsylvania and the Jerseys, with the men

---

officers were buried at a short distance from their general, but without coffins, and in the military manner. All the gravel were within the walls of the city, and near the Port of St. Louis.

These particulars were communicated to me by Mr. William Smith of Quebec, who had received them from several persons acquainted with them at the time, and especially from Mr. Thompson, who assisted at the burial of Montgomery, and who pointed out the place of his grave a few years ago, when his remains were taken up and removed to New York.

already sent off by Colonel Warner, these misfortunes will be done away, and things will resume a more favorable and promising appearance than ever.

I need not mention to you the great importance of this place, and the consequent possession of all Canada, in the scale of American affairs. You are well apprized of it. To whomsoever it belongs, in their favor, probably, will the balance turn. If it is in ours, success I think will most certainly crown our virtuous struggles. If it is in theirs, the contest at best will be doubtful, hazardous, and bloody. The glorious work must be accomplished in the course of this winter, otherwise it will become difficult, most probably impracticable; for administration, knowing that it will be impossible ever to reduce us to a state of slavery and arbitrary rule without it, will certainly send a large reinforcement thither in the spring. I am fully convinced, that your exertions will be invariably directed to this grand object, and I already view the approaching day, when you and your brave followers will enter this important fortress, with every honor attendant on victory. Then will you have added the only link wanting in the great chain of Continental union, and render the freedom of your country secure.

Wishing you a speedy recovery, and the possession of those laurels, which your bravery and perseverance justly merit, I am, dear Sir, yours, &c. [10]

---

[10] Arnold wrote from Quebec, on the 27th of February, in reply to this letter, and seemed in high spirits, though encompassed with innumerable difficulties. His mind was of so elastic a nature, that the more it was pressed, the greater was its power of resistance. Congress had recently promoted him to the rank of brigadier-general, as a reward for his good conduct, during the perilous enterprise in which he had been engaged from the time he left Cambridge, till he was wounded in the unsuccessful assault on Quebec. "The severity of the climate," he observes, "the troops very ill clad and worse paid, the trouble of reconciling matters among the inhabitants, and lately an uneasiness among some

To Joseph Reed, Cambridge, 31 January, 1776

Dear Sir,

In my last, by Mr. John Adams, I communicated my distresses to you on account of my want of your assistance. I have since been under some concern at having done it, lest it should precipitate your return before you are ready for it, or bring on a final resignation, which I am unwilling to think of, if your return can be made convenient and agreeable. True it is, that from a variety of

of the New York and other officers, who think themselves neglected in the new arrangement, while those who deserted the cause and went home last fall have been promoted; in short, the choice of difficulties I have had to encounter has rendered affairs so very perplexing, that I have often been at a loss how to conduct them." He alludes here, and perhaps with some justice, to the case of Colonel Enos, and his officers, who deserted him in the wilderness on their way to Canada, but who were nevertheless retained and promoted in the new establishment.

causes my business has been, and now is, multiplied and perplexed; whilst the means of execution are greatly contracted. This may be a cause for my wishing you here, but no inducement to your coming, if you hesitated before.

I have now to thank you for your favors, and for the several articles of intelligence, which they convey. The account given of your navy, at the same time that it is exceedingly unfavorable to our wishes, is a little provoking to me, inasmuch as it has deprived us of necessary articles, which otherwise would have been sent hither; but which a kind of fatality I fear will for ever deprive us of. [11] In the instance of New York, we are not to receive a particle of what you expected would be sent from thence; the time and season passing away, as I believe the

---

[11] Armed vessels were now fitting out in Philadelphia by order of the Continental Congress, under the command of Commodore Hopkins.

troops in Boston also will, before the season for taking the field arrives. I dare say they are preparing for it now, as we have undoubted intelligence of Clinton's leaving Boston with a number of troops, believed to be designed for Long Island, or New York, in consequence of assurances from Governor Tryon of powerful aid from the Tories there.

I hope my countrymen of Virginia will rise superior to any losses the whole navy of Great Britain can bring on them, and that the destruction of Norfolk, and the attempted devastation of other places, will have no other effect, than to unite the whole country in one indissoluble bond. A few more of such flaming arguments, as were exhibited at Falmouth and Norfolk,[12] added to the sound doctrine and unanswerable reasoning contained in the pamphlet

---

[12] The town of Norfolk, in Virginia, had been bombarded and burnt by Lord Dunmore on the 1st of January.

"*Common Sense,*" will not leave numbers at a loss to decide upon the propriety of a separation.

By a letter of the 21st instant from General Wooster, I find, that Arnold was continuing the blockade of Quebec on the 19th, which, under the heaviness of our loss there, is a most favorable circumstance, and exhibits a fresh proof of Arnold's ability and perseverance in the midst of difficulties. The reinforcement ordered to him will, I hope, complete the entire conquest of Canada this winter; and except for the loss of the gallant chief, and his brave followers, I should think the rebuff rather favorable than otherwise; for had the country been subdued by such a handful of men, it is more than probable, that it would have been left to the defence of a few, and rescued from us in the spring. Our eyes will now be open not only to the importance of holding it, but to the numbers which are requisite to that end.

In my last I think I informed you of my sending General Lee to New York, with the intention of securing the Tories on Long Island, and preventing, if possible, the King's troops from making a lodgment there; but I fear the Congress will be duped by the representations from that government, or yield to them in such a manner as to become marplots to the expedition. The city seems to be entirely under the government of Tryon and the captain of the man-of-war.

Mrs. Washington desires me to thank you for the picture sent her. Mr. Campbell, whom I never saw, to my knowledge, has made a very formidable figure of the Commander-in-chief; giving him a sufficient portion of terror in his countenance. Mrs. Washington also desires her compliments to Mrs. Reed, as I do, and, with the sincerest regard and affection, I remain, dear Sir, your most obedient servant.

P. S. I had written the letter herewith enclosed before your favor of the 21st came to hand. The account given of the behaviour of the men under General Montgomery, is exactly consonant to the opinion I have formed of these people, and such as they will exhibit abundant proofs of, in similar cases whenever called upon. Place them behind a parapet, a breast-work, stone wall, or any thing that will afford them shelter, and, from their knowledge of a firelock, they will give a good account of the enemy; but I am as well convinced, as if I had seen it, that they will not march boldly up to a work, nor stand exposed in a plain; and yet, if we are furnished with the means, and the weather will afford us a passage, and we can get in men, for these three things are necessary, something must be attempted. The men must be brought to face danger; they cannot always have an entrenchment or a stone wall as a safeguard or shield; and it is of essential importance, that the troops in Boston should be destroyed if possible before they can be reinforced or removed. This is clearly my opinion. Whether circumstances will admit of the trial, and, if tried, what will be the result, the All-wise Disposer of events alone can tell.

To the President of Congress, Cambridge, 9 February, 1776

Sir,

The purport of this letter will be directed to a single object. Through you I mean to lay it before Congress, and, at the same time that I beg their serious attention to the subject, to ask pardon for intruding an opinion, not only unasked, but, in some measure, repugnant to their resolves.

The disadvantages attending the limited enlistment of troops are too apparent to those, who are eyewitnesses of them, to render any animadversions necessary; but to gentlemen at a distance, whose attention is engrossed by a thousand important objects, the case may be otherwise. That this cause precipitated the fate of the brave and much-to-be-lamented General Montgomery, and

brought on the defeat, which followed thereupon, I have not the most distant doubt;
for, had he not been apprehensive of the
troops leaving him at so important a crisis,
but continued the blockade of Quebec, a
capitulation, from the best accounts I have
been able to collect, must inevitably have
followed. And that we were not at one time
obliged to dispute these lines, under disad-
vantageous circumstances, proceeding from
the same cause, to wit, the troops disbanding
of themselves before the militia could be got
in, is to me a matter of wonder and aston-
ishment, and proves, that General Howe was
either unacquainted with our situation, or
restrained by his instructions from putting
any thing to hazard, till his reinforcements
should arrive.

The instance of General Montgomery
(I mention it, because it is a striking one,
for a number of others might be adduced)
proves, that, instead of having men to take

advantage of circumstances, you are in a manner compelled, right or wrong, to make circumstances yield to a secondary consideration. Since the 1st of December, I have been devising every means in my power to secure these encampments; and though I am sensible that we never have, since that period, been able to act upon the offensive, and at times not in a condition to defend, yet the cost of marching home one set of men, bringing in another, the havoc and waste occasioned by the first, the repairs necessary for the second, with a thousand incidental charges and inconveniences, which have arisen, and which it is scarce possible either to recollect or describe, amount to near as much, as the keeping up a respectable body of troops the whole time, ready for any emergency, would have done. To this may be added, that you never can have a well disciplined army.

To bring men to be well acquainted with the duties of a soldier, requires time.

To bring them under proper discipline and subordination, not only requires time, but is a work of great difficulty, and, in this army, where there is so little distinction between the officers and soldiers, requires an uncommon degree of attention. To expect, then, the same service from raw and undisciplined recruits, as from veteran soldiers, is to expect what never did and perhaps never will happen. Men, who are familiarized to danger, meet it without shrinking; whereas troops unused to service often apprehend danger where no danger is. Three things prompt men to a regular discharge of their duty in time of action; natural bravery, hope of reward, and fear of punishment. The two first are common to the untutored and the disciplined soldier; but the last most obviously distinguishes the one from the other. A coward, when taught to believe, that, if he breaks his ranks and abandons his colors, he will be punished with death by his own party, will take his chance against the enemy; but a man, who thinks little of the one, and is fearful of the other, acts from present feelings, regardless of consequences.

Again, men of a day's standing will not look forward; and from experience we find, that, as the time approaches for their discharge, they grow careless of their arms, ammunition, and camp utensils. Nay, even the barracks themselves have felt uncommon marks of wanton depredation, and lay us under fresh trouble and additional expense in providing for every fresh set, when we find it next to impossible to procure such articles, as are absolutely necessary in the first instance. To this may be added the seasoning, which new recruits must have to a camp, and the loss consequent thereupon. But this is not all. Men engaged for a short and limited time only, have the officers too much in their power; for, to obtain a degree of popularity in order to induce a second enlistment, a kind of familiarity takes place, which brings on a relaxation of discipline, unlicensed furloughs, and other indulgences incompatible with order and good government; by which means the latter part of the time, for which the soldier was engaged, is spent in undoing what you were aiming to inculcate in the first.

To go into an enumeration of all the evils we have experienced, in this late great change of the army, and the expenses incidental to it, to say nothing of the hazard we have run, and must run, between the discharging of one army and enlistment of another, unless an enormous expense of militia is incurred, would greatly exceed the bounds of a letter. What I have already taken the liberty of saying will serve to convey a general idea of the matter; and therefore I shall, with all due deference, take the freedom to give it as my opinion, that, if the Congress have any reason to believe, that there will be occasion for troops another year, and consequently for another enlistment, they would save money, and have infinitely better troops, if they were, even at a bounty of twenty, thirty, or more dollars, to engage the men already enlisted till January next, and such others as may be wanted to complete the establishment, for and during the war. I will not undertake to say, that the men can be had upon these terms; but I am satisfied, that it will never do to let the matter alone, as it was last year, till the time of service was near expiring. The hazard is too great, in the first place; in the next, the trouble and perplexity of disbanding one army and raising another at the same instant, and in such a critical situation as the last was, are scarcely in the power of words to describe, and such as no man, who has experienced them once, will ever undergo again.

If Congress should differ from me in sentiment upon this point, I have only to beg that they will do me the justice to believe, that I have nothing more in view, than what to me appears necessary to advance the public weal, although in the first instance it will be attended with a capital expense; and that I have the honor to be, &c.

PART 3:

1777

July–December

We should never despair, our Situation before has been unpromising and has changed for the better, so I trust, it will again. If new difficulties arise, we must only put forth New Exertions and proportion our Efforts to the exigency of the times.

To Major-General Schuyler, Head-Quarters, Ramapo, 24 July, 1777

Dear Sir,

Your two favors of the 21st and 22d instant with their enclosures are come to hand. I am sorry to find, that you have not yet been joined by a large number of militia, and that it has been found necessary to dismiss a part even of those, who have come to your assistance, though their presence is at this time so urgently wanted. I hope, however, that your situation will soon be far more respectable; as I cannot but think the eastern States, which are so intimately concerned in the matter, will exert themselves to throw in effectual succors to enable you to check the progress of the enemy, and repel a danger, with which they are so immediately threatened. The information of the prisoners and others, transmitted by you, does not make the numbers of the enemy to exceed the idea first entertained of them, nor do I see any thing in it to induce a belief, that their progress will be so rapid, as not to give you time to make proper preparations and receive sufficient accessions of force to enable you to give them a vigorous and successful opposition. They do not appear to be much more than five thousand strong, and seem to be unprovided with wagons to transport the immense quantity of baggage and warlike apparatus, without which they cannot pretend to penetrate the country. You mention their having a great number of horses; but they will nevertheless require a considerable number of wagons, for there are a great many things that cannot be transported on horses. As they can never think of advancing, without securing their rear by leaving garrisons in the fortresses behind, the force with which they can come against you will be greatly reduced by the detachments necessary for the purpose. And as they have to cut out their road, and remove the impediments you have put in the way, this circumstance, with the incumbrance they must feel in their baggage, will inevitably retard their march a considerable time, and give you leisure and opportunity to prepare a good reception for them. If they continue to act in detachments, you will have it in your power to improve it to very great advantage, by falling vigorously upon some one of them with your whole force, which, if you are fortunate enough to succeed in, will be fatal to them.

I have directed General Lincoln to repair to you as speedily as the state of his health, which is not very perfect, will permit him.

This gentleman has always supported the character of a judicious, brave, active officer, and as he is exceedingly popular and much respected in the State of Massachusetts, to which he belongs, he will have a degree of influence over the militia, which cannot fail of being very advantageous. I have destined him more particularly to the command of them, and I promise myself it will have a powerful tendency to make them turn out with more cheerfulness, and to inspire them with perseverance to remain in the field, and fortitude and spirit to do their duty while in it. The confidence they have in him will certainly go a great way towards producing these desirable ends. You intimate the propriety of having a body of men stationed somewhere about the Grants. The expediency of such a measure appears to me evident; for it would certainly make General Burgoyne very circumspect in his advances, if it did not totally prevent them. It would keep him in continual anxiety for his rear, and oblige him to leave the posts behind him much stronger than he would otherwise do, and would answer many other valuable purposes. General Lincoln could not be more serviceable, than in command of this body, and no person could be more proper for it.

From the view I have of the matter, I should also think it necessary to send General Arnold, or some other sensible, spirited officer to Fort Schuyler, to take care of that post, keep up the spirits of the inhabitants, and cultivate and improve the favorable disposition of the Indians. This is recommended on the supposition, that any thing formidable should appear in that quarter.

I am, dear Sir, &c.

To Governor Trumbull, Coryell's Ferry, 31 July, 1777

Sir,

I was just now honored with your letter of the 25th instant. The evacuation of Ticonderoga and Mount Independence was an event so unexpected; that I do not wonder it should produce in the minds of the people, at least the well attached, the effects you mention. I am entirely in sentiment with you, that the cause, leading to this unhappy measure, should be fully and minutely examined. Public justice, on the one hand, demands it, if it was not the result of prudence and necessity; and, on the other, the reputation of the officers concerned, if they are not blameworthy. Had not Congress considered that as a separate department, appointed the officers in some instances to that command themselves, and been fully possessed of all the facts that I am respecting the events, I should not have doubted a single moment about directing an inquiry. These matters, I say, have laid me under some doubts as to the line I should pursue; but I am persuaded, that an examination will be ordered in a few days, either by the Congress or myself, when I hope the subject will be properly discussed, and that done which is right.

As to sending Continental troops from Peekskill, no more can be detached from thence to the northern army, than are already gone. Two brigades, Nixon's and Glover's, have been ordered from thence to their aid; more than were ever intended in the arrangement of our forces. Not a man more can go, as all the Continental troops at that post, excepting two thousand, are called to join this army. For I have to inform you, that General Howe's object and operations no longer remain a secret. At half after nine o'clock this morning, I received an express from Congress, advising that the enemy's fleet, consisting of two hundred and twenty-eight sail, were at the Capes of Delaware yesterday in the forenoon. This being the case, there can be no doubt but he will make a vigorous push to possess Philadelphia, and we should collect all the force we can to oppose him.

Fearing from report and from the event itself (the abandonment of the northern posts), that distrust, jealousy, and suspicion of the conduct of the officers might arise in the militia, and that degree of confidence in them wanted, which would be necessary to success, and to give a more promising aspect to our affairs in that quarter, I sent Generals Lincoln and Arnold to assist in that command. These two gentlemen are esteemed good officers, and I think very deservedly. I am persuaded, that nothing their judgments shall direct will be omitted to stop the progress of General Burgoyne's arms, so far as in them lies; and I am equally sure, that their personal exertions and bravery will not be wanting in any instance. Their presence I trust will remove every ground of diffidence and backwardness in the militia, and that they will go on, when and where their services are demanded, with a spirit and resolution becoming freemen and the sacred cause in which they are engaged. As the troops are on their march from hence, I shall not add more, than that I have the most entire confidence in your exertions upon every occasion to advance the common interest; and that I have the honor to be, with great respect, Sir, &c. [13]

---

[13] The appointment of the Marquis de Lafayette as a major-general in the service of the United States, one of the most important events of the revolution, took place on the 31st or July, and is thus recorded in the Journals of Congress.

"Whereas the Marquis de Lafayette, out of his great zeal to the cause of liberty, in which the United State are engaged, has left his family and connexions, and at his own expense come over to offer his services to the United States, without pension or particular allowance, and is anxious to risk his life in our cause; Resolved, that his service be accepted, and that, in consideration of his zeal, his illustrious family, and connexions, he have the rank and commission of major-general in the army of the United States."

To Governor George Clinton, Head-
Quarters, 15 October, 1777

Dear Sir,

I was this day honored with yours of the
9th, containing a full account of the storm
of Forts Montgomery and Clinton. General
Putnam had given me information of the loss
two days before, but not in so full and ample
a manner. It is to be regretted, that so brave
a resistance did not meet with a suitable
reward. You have however the satisfaction
of knowing, that every thing was done, that
could possibly be done by a handful against
a far superior force. This I am convinced
was the case. This affair might have been
attended with fatal consequences, had not
there been a most Providential interven-
tion in favor of General Gates's arms on
the 7th instant; but I am fully of opinion,
that Sir Henry Clinton will not advance
much farther up the river, upon hearing of

Burgoyne's defeat and retreat. Nothing but an absolute necessity could have induced me to withdraw any further part of the troop allotted for the defence of the posts up the North River; but such was the reduced state of our Continental regiments, after the battle of Brandywine, and such the difficulty of procuring reinforcements of militia from the southward, that without the troops from Peekskill we should scarcely have been able to keep the field against General Howe. I had the greatest hopes, that General Putnam would draw in as many Connecticut militia, as would replace the Continental troops, and I make no doubt but he did all in his power to obtain them in time. I am sorry that you were under the necessity of destroying the frigates. The only consolation is, that if we had not done it ourselves, the enemy would either have done it for us, or have carried them down for their own use. [14]

---

[14] For other particulars respecting the capture of Forts Montgomery and Clinton.

Since the battle of Germantown, the two armies have remained in a manner quiet. The enemy have made several attempts to remove the obstructions in the Delaware, but hitherto without effect. They are now making preparations to raise batteries in the rear of Fort Miffin, which commands the uppermost chevaux-de-frise. If we can maintain that post, and one opposite upon the Jersey shore, I hope our ships, galleys, and floating batteries, will be able to keep their stations and repel any force, that can be brought by water directly in front. I most earnestly wait for further news from the northward, which I hope will bring us accounts of the total ruin of Burgoyne's army.

It is not unlikely that one of Sir Henry Clinton's objects will be to destroy the boats and small craft in the North River. Should this be the case, and he succeed, I think it will be advisable to set a number of workmen to building fiat-bottomed boats at some secure places within three or four miles of the water, from which they may be easily hauled. They are so exceedingly useful, and so frequently wanted, that I think the business cannot, in such case, be too soon begun carried on with too much expedition. I have written to General Putnam upon the same subject. I am, dear Sir, &c.

To Richard Henry Lee, in Congress, Matuchen Hill, 17 October, 1777

Dear Sir,

Your favor of the 5th instant, as also that of the 11th by Baron de Kalb, are both at hand. It is not in my power at present to answer your query respecting the appointment of this gentleman. But, Sir, if there is any thing in a report, that Congress have appointed, or as others say are about to appoint, Brigadier Conway a major-general in this army, it will be as unfortunate a measure as ever was adopted. I may add, and I think with truth, that it will give a fatal blow to the existence of the army. Upon so interesting a subject, I must speak plainly. The duty I owe my country, the ardent desire I have to promote its true interests, and justice to individuals, require this of me. General Conway's merit, then, as an officer, and his importance in this army, exist more in his own imagination, than in reality. For it is a maxim with him, to leave no service of his own untold, nor to want any thing, which is to be obtained by importunity.

But as I do not mean to detract from him any merit he possesses, and only wish to have the matter taken upon its true ground, after allowing him every thing that his warmest friends would contend for, I would ask, why the youngest brigadier in the service (for I believe he is so) should be put over the heads of all the eldest, and thereby take rank of, and command gentlemen, who but yesterday were his seniors; gentlemen, who, I will be bold to say, in behalf of some of them at least, are of sound judgment and unquestionable bravery? If there was a degree of conspicuous merit in General Conway, unpossessed by any of his seniors, the confusion, which might be occasioned by it, would stand warranted upon the principles of sound policy; for I readily agree, that this is no time for trifling; but, at the same time that I cannot subscribe to the fact, this truth I am very well assured of (though I have not directly, nor indirectly, exchanged a word with anyone of the brigadiers on the subject, nor am I certain that anyone has heard of the appointment), that they will not serve under him. I leave you to guess, therefore, at the situation this army would be in at so important a crisis, if this event should take place. These gentlemen have feelings as officers; and though they do not dispute the authority of Congress to make appointments, they will judge of the propriety of acting under them.

In a word, the service is so difficult, and every necessary so expensive, that almost all our officers are tired out. Do not, therefore, afford them good pretexts for retiring. No day passes over my head without application for leave to resign. Within the last six days, I am certain, twenty commissions at least have been tendered to me. I must, therefore, conjure you to conjure Congress to consider this matter well, and not, by a real act of injustice, compel some good officers to leave the service, and thereby incur a train of evils unforeseen and irremediable. To sum up the whole, I have been a slave to the service; I have undergone more than most men are aware of to harmonize so many discordant parts; but it will be impossible for me to be of any further service, if such insuperable difficulties are thrown in my way. You may believe me, my good Sir, that I have no earthly views, but the public good, in what I have said. I have no prejudice against General Conway, nor desire to serve any other brigadier, further than I think the cause will be benefited by it; to bring which to a speedy and happy conclusion, is the most fervent wish of my soul.[15]

With respect to the wants of the militia, in the articles of clothing, you must be well convinced, that it is not in my power to supply them in the smallest degree, when near one half of our own men are rendered unfit for service for want of these things. I can add no more at present, than that I am, dear Sir, &c.

To Baron D'Arendt, Head-Quarters, 18 October, 1777

Sir,

Being recovered from the indisposition under which you lately labored, you are to proceed immediately to Fort Mifflin on Mud Island and take the command of the troops there, and those which may be sent. I shall not prescribe any particular line for your conduct, because I repose the utmost confidence in your bravery, knowledge, and judgment; and because the mode of defence must depend on a variety of circumstances, which will be best known to those, who are on the spot. I will add, that the maintenance of this post is of the last importance to the States of America, and that preventing the enemy from obtaining possession of it, under the smiles of Heaven, will be the means of our defeating the army to which we are now opposed; or of obliging them disgracefully to abandon the city of Philadelphia, which is now in their hands.

I have detached to-day a further reinforcement to the garrison, and have instructed Colonel Greene, who commands at Red Bank, to cooperate with you, and to render you every assistance in his power. You will maintain with him, and with Commodore Hazelwood, who commands our fleet, a good understanding and the strictest harmony. These will be essential; and, by mutually aiding each other, I shall look forward for the most happy events. You will be particularly attentive to the state of your ammunition and provision, advising me of the same from time to time, and of such supplies as you may judge necessary to be sent to you. You will also report to me the situation of the garrison, as often as it shall be requisite, and will not fail to transmit to me frequent and the most early intelligence of every important occurrence. I recommend your utmost despatch to arrive at the garrison; and you have my warmest wishes, that the command may prove honorable to yourself and beneficial to America. I am, &c.[16]

16 The Baron d' Arendt was a colonel in the Continental service, and had been appointed on the 19th of March to the command of the German Battalion.

To the President of Congress, Head-Quarters, Whitemarsh, 10 December, 1777

Sir,

I have the honor to inform you, that in the course of last week, from a variety of intelligence, I had reason to expect that General Howe was preparing to give us a general action. Accordingly, on Thursday night he moved from the city with all his force, except a very inconsiderable part left in his lines and redoubts, and appeared the next morning on Chestnut Hill, in front of, and about three miles distant from, our right wing. As soon as their position was discovered, the Pennsylvania militia were ordered from our right, to skirmish with their light advanced parties; and I am sorry to mention, that Brigadier-General Irvine, who led them on, had the misfortune to be wounded and to be made prisoner. Nothing more occurred on that day.

On Friday night the enemy changed their ground, and moved to our left, within a mile of our line, where they remained quiet and advantageously posted the whole of the next day. On Sunday they inclined still further to our left; and, from every appearance, there was reason to apprehend they were determined on an action. In this movement, their advanced and flanking parties were warmly attacked by Colonel Morgan and his corps, and also by the Maryland militia under Colonel Gist. Their loss I cannot ascertain; but I am informed it was considerable, having regard to the number of the corps who engaged them. About sunset, after various marches and countermarches, they halted; and I still supposed, from their disposition and preceding maneuvers, that they would attack us in the night or early the next morning; but in this I was mistaken. On Monday afternoon they began to move again, and, instead of advancing, filed off from their right; and the first certain account that I could obtain of their intentions was, that they were in full march towards Philadelphia by two or three routes. I immediately detached light parties after them to fall upon their rear; but they were not able to come up with them.

The enemy's loss, as I have observed, I cannot ascertain. One account from the city is, that five hundred wounded had been sent in; another is, that eighty-two wagons had gone in with men in this situation. These, I fear, are both exaggerated, and not to be depended upon. We lost twenty-seven men in Morgan's corps, killed and wounded, besides Major Morris, a brave and gallant officer, who is among the latter. Of the Maryland militia there were also sixteen or seventeen wounded. I have not received further returns yet. I sincerely wish that they had made an attack; as the issue, in all probability, from the disposition of our troops, and the strong situation of our camp, would have been fortunate and happy. At the same time I must add, that reason, prudence, and every principle of policy, forbade us from quitting our post to attack them. Nothing but success would have justified the measure; and this could not be expected from their position.

The constant attention and watching I was obliged to give the enemy's movements would not allow me to write before; and this I believe was the less material, as I have reason to think your committee, who were in camp most of the time, and who are now here, transmitted an account of such occurrences as they deemed important in any degree. The first cause, too, Sir, and my engagements with the committee previous to the coming out of the enemy, will, I trust, sufficiently apologize for my not acknowledging before the honor of your favors or the 13th ultimo and the 1st instant, which came to hand in due order and time. I have the honor to be, &c.

To the President of Congress, Head-Quarters, near the Gulf, 14 December, 1777

Sir,

On Thursday evening I bad the honor to receive your favor of the 8th instant. From several letters, which have lately passed between General Howe and myself; I am fully convinced, that any propositions by me to release the Baron St. Ouary from captivity, either by an exchange or on parole, would be unavailing. He has explicitly stated his sentiments, and has declared himself to be utterly against a partial exchange. The situation of the Baron, through the interest and acquaintance of the Marquis de Lafayette with an officer in the guards, is much more comfortable than that of any of our officers, who are prisoners, he being on parole in the city, whilst they are all confined in the State-House. I do not know that it is the practice in Europe not to consider volunteers as prisoners. I am inclined to believe that it is not, and that they are generally held as such, unless the contrary is particularly stipulated by cartel. However this may be, they have been held in the present contest on both sides on the footing of other prisoners, and exchanged as such. Besides this, I fear that a proposition calculated for the peculiar benefit of the Baron, would be ill received by our unhappy officers, who have been much longer in confinement, whose sufferings are far greater than his, and who claim a right to exchange in due course. [17]

---

[17] In their resolve, respecting the Baron St. Ouary, Congress designated him as "a gallant gentleman from France, engaged as a volunteer in the service of the United States, and lately by the fortune of war made prisoner by the British." They instructed General Washington to apply for bill release, on the ground that volunteers were not to be reported as prisoners of war; but, if General Howe should not accede to the doctrine, then an enlargement by exchange or on parole was to be solicited for the Baron St. Ouary.—*Journals, December 3d*

The inquiries, directed in the resolutions contained in your letter of the 30th ultimo, respecting the loss of the forts in the Highlands and of Fort Mifflin, I shall order to be made, as soon as circumstances will admit. These, however, it is probable, will not be effected in a short time, from the situation of our affairs and inevitable necessity. On Thursday morning we marched from our old encampment, and intended to pass the Schuylkill at Matson's Ford, where a bridge had been laid across the river. When the first division and a part of the second had passed, they found a body of the enemy, consisting, from the best accounts we have been able to obtain, of four thousand men, under Lord Cornwallis, possessing themselves of the heights on both sides of the road leading from the river and the defile called the Gulf, which I presume are well known to some part of your honorable body. This unexpected event obliged such of our troops, as had crossed, to repass, and prevented our getting over till the succeeding night. This maneuver on the part of the enemy was not in consequence of any information they had of our movement, but was designed to secure the pass whilst they were foraging in the neighbouring country. They were met in their advance by General Potter, with part of the Pennsylvania militia, who behaved with bravery and gave them every possible opposition, till he was obliged to retreat from their superior numbers. Had we been an hour sooner, or had the least information of the measure, I am persuaded we should have given his Lordship a fortunate stroke, or obliged him to return without effecting his purpose, or drawn out all General Howe's force to support him. Our first intelligence was, that it was all out. Lord Cornwallis collected a good deal of forage, and returned to the city the night we passed the river. No discrimination marked his proceedings. All property, whether of friends or foes, that came in their way, was seized and carried off.

Enclosed is a copy of a letter from General Burgoyne, by which you will perceive he requests leave to embark his troops at Rhode Island, or at some place on the Sound; and, in case this cannot be granted, that he may be allowed, with his suite, to go there and return from thence to England. His first proposition, as I have observed upon a former occasion, is certainly inadmissible, and for reasons obvious to himself. As to the second, which respects the departure of himself and suite, Congress will be pleased to determine upon it and favor me with their sentiments by the first opportunity, that I may know what answer to give him.[18]

---

[18] "*In Congress, December 17th*; Resolved, that General Washington be directed to inform General Burgoyne, that Congress will not receive nor consider any proposition for indulgence or altering the terms of the convention of Saratoga, unless immediately directed to

I learn from. Mr. Griffin, who has just come from Boston, that this gentleman either holds, or professes to hold, very different ideas of our power from what he formerly entertained; that, without reserve, he has said it would be next to impossible for Britain to succeed in her views, and that he should with freedom declare his sentiments accordingly on his arrival in England; and that he seemed to think the recognition of our independence by the King and Parliament an eligible measure, under a treaty of commerce upon a large and extensive scale. How far these professions are founded in sincerity, it is not easy to determine; but if they are, what a mighty change! While I am on the subject of Mr. Burgoyne and his army, I would submit it to Congress, whether it will not be right and reasonable,

their own body." Congress had already voted, that a proposal for shipping the troops from any other place, than that stipulated in the convention of Saratoga, should be rejected. —December 1st.

that all expenses, incurred on their account for provisions, should be paid and satisfied previously to their embarkation and departure; I mean by an actual deposit of the money. Unless this is done, there will be little reason to suppose, that it will ever be paid. They have failed (that is, the nation) in other instances, as I have been told, after liquidating their accounts and giving the fullest certificates, and we cannot expect they will keep better faith with us than with others. The payment too, I should apprehend, ought to be in coin, as it will enable us to administer some relief to our unfortunate officers and men who are in captivity.

December 15th.—Congress seem to have taken for granted a fact, that is really not so. All the forage for the army has been constantly drawn from Bucks and Philadelphia counties, and those parts most contiguous to the city; insomuch that it was nearly exhausted, and entirely so in the country below our camp. From these, too, were obtained all the supplies of flour, that circumstances would admit of. The millers in most instances were unwilling to grind, either from their disaffection or from motives of fear. This made the supplies less than they otherwise might have been, and the quantity, which was drawn from thence was little, besides what the guards, placed at the mills, compelled them to manufacture. As to stock, I do not know that much was had from thence, nor do I know that any considerable supply could have been had.

I confess I have felt myself greatly embarrassed with respect to a vigorous exercise of military power. An ill-placed humanity, perhaps, and a reluctance to give distress, may have restrained me too far; but these were not all. I have been well aware of the prevalent jealousy of military power, and that this has been considered as an evil, much to be apprehended, even by the best and most sensible among us. Under this idea, I have been cautious, and wished to avoid as much as possible any act that might increase it. However, Congress may be assured, that no exertions of mine, as far as circumstances will admit, shall be wanting to provide our own troops with supplies on the one hand, and to prevent the enemy from getting them on the other. At the same time they must be apprized, that many obstacles have arisen to render the former more precarious and difficult than they usually were, from a change in the commissary's department, at a very critical and interesting period. I should be happy, if the civil authority in the several States, through the recommendations of Congress, or their own mere will, seeing the necessity of supporting the army, would always adopt the most spirited measures, suited to the end. The people at large are governed much by custom. To acts of legislation or civil authority they have ever been taught to yield a willing obedience, without reasoning about their propriety; on those of military power, whether immediate or derived originally from another source, they have ever looked with a jealous and suspicious eye. I have the honor to be, &c.[19]

[19] Mr. Lee replied;—"I was a good deal surprised to find you had been told Congress had appointed General Conway a major-general. No such appointment has been made, nor do I believe it will, whilst it is likely to produce the evil consequences you suggest. It is very true, that, both within and without doors, there have been advocates for the measure, and it has been affirmed, that it would be very agreeable to the army, whose favorite Mr. Conway was asserted to be. My judgment on this business was not formed until I received your letter. I am very sure Congress would not take

any step that might injure the army, or even have a tendency that way; and I verily believe they wish to lessen your difficulties by every means in their power, from an entire conviction that the purest motives of public good direct your actions.

"The business of a Board of War is so extensive, so important, and demanding such constant attention, that Congress see clearly the necessity of constituting a new board, out of Congress, whose time shall be entire devoted to that new essential department. It is by some warmly proposed, that this board shall be filled by the three following gentlemen, Colonel Reed, Colonel Pickering, the present adjutant-general, and Colonel Harrison, your secretary; and that General Conway be appointed adjutant-general in the room of Colonel Pickering. It is my wish, and I am sure it is so of many others, to know your full and candid sentiments on this subject. For my own part, I cannot be satisfied with giving any opinion on the point, until I am favored with your sentiments, which I shall be much obliged to you for, Sir, as soon as your time will permit.

"It has been affirmed, that General Conway would quit the service, if he were not made a major-general. But I have been told in confidence, that he would leave it at the end of this campaign if he was appointed, unless his word of honor were taken to continue for any fixed time. And it is a question with me, whether the advocates for General Conway will not miss their aim, if he should be appointed adjutant-general, unless he has the rank of major-general also. My reason for thinking so is, that I have been informed General Conway desires to retire to his family, provided he can carry from this country home with him a rank that will raise him in France. It is very certain that the public good demands a speedy erecting and the judicious filling of the new Board of War, and I sincerely wish it may be done in the most proper manner. I do not imagine Congress would appoint Colonel Harrison, without first knowing whether you could spare him; nor do I think that so important an office, as that of adjutant-general, should be touched without the maturest consideration." —*MS Letter, October 20th.*

Not withstanding the strong representations of General Washington in the above letter to Mr. Lee, and the decided opinions expressed in Mr. Lee's reply, General Conway was appointed by Congress a few weeks afterwards inspector-general of the army, and raised to the rank of major-general over several older brigadier-generals.—*Journals, December 13th.*

PART 4:

1778

February–July

If we desire to avoid insult, we must be able to repel it; if we desire to secure peace, one of the most powerful instruments of our rising prosperity, it must be known, that we are at all times ready for War.

An Address to the Inhabitants of New Jersey, Pennsylvania, Delaware, Maryland, and Virginia, Valley Forge, 18 February, 1778

Friends, Countrymen, and Fellow Citizens,

After three campaigns, during which the brave subjects of these States have contended, not unsuccessfully, with one of the most powerful kingdoms upon earth, we now find ourselves at least upon a level with our opponents; and there is the best reason to believe, that efforts adequate to the abilities of this country would enable us speedily to conclude the war, and to secure the invaluable blessings of peace, liberty, and safety. With this view, it is in contemplation, at the opening of the next campaign, to assemble a force sufficient, not barely to cover the country from a repetition of those depredations which it has already suffered, but also to operate offensively, and to strike some decisive blow.

In the prosecution of this object, it is to be feared that so large an army may suffer for want of provisions. The distance between this and the eastern States, whence considerable supplies of flesh have been hitherto drawn, will necessarily render those supplies extremely precarious. And unless the virtuous yeomanry of New Jersey, Pennsylvania, Delaware, Maryland, and Virginia, will exert themselves to prepare cattle for the use of the many during the months of May, June, and July next, great difficulties may arise in the course of the campaign.

It is therefore recommended to the inhabitants of those States, to put up and feed immediately as many of their stock cattle as they can spare, so that they may be driven to this army within that period. A bountiful price will be given, and the proprietors may assure themselves, that they will render a most essential service to the illustrious cause of their country, and contribute in a great degree to shorten this bloody contest. But should there be any so insensible to the common interest, as not to exert themselves upon these generous principles, the private interest of those, whose situation makes them liable to become immediate subjects to the enemy's incursions, should prompt them at least to a measure, which is calculated to save their property from plunder, their families from insult, and their own persons from abuse, hopeless confinement, or perhaps a violent death.

To Governor Livingston, Valley Forge,
14 March, 1778

Sir,

I have the honor of yours of the 2d instant;
and, I can assure you, I feel myself very
sensibly affected by the strenuous manner in
which you express the public regard of the
State and your personal friendship towards
me. I only desire to be the object of both,
while in your good opinion and that of the
public I continue to merit them.

We seem hitherto to have mistaken each
other, in respect to the troop of light horse.
I did not mean to enlist them into the Continental service, but only to engage them for
a few months, while the Continental horse
were recruiting, upon the same terms that
I engaged the Morris County horse last
winter. It will be expected, that they provide

their own horses, arms, and accoutrements, and be paid accordingly. If Captain Arnold will come into the service upon the above terms, I will immediately take him into employ. It is impossible to devise any other mode of disposing of deserters, than to let them go at large among us, provided there is no particular cause of suspicion against them. To confine them would effectually put a stop to a drain, which weakens the enemy more, in the course of a year, than you would imagine. I am pleased with the favorable account you give of Count Pulaski's conduct while at Trenton. He is a gentleman of great activity and unquestionable bravery, and only wants a fuller knowledge of our language and customs to make him a valuable officer. I am, &c.

To the President of Congress, Head-Quarters, Valley Forge, 3 April, 1778

Sir,

Captain Lee of the light dragoons, and the officers under his command, having uniformly distinguished themselves by a conduct of exemplary zeal, prudence, and bravery, I took occasion, on a late signal instance of it, to express the high sense entertained of their merit, and to assure him, that it should not fail of being properly noticed. I was induced to give this assurance from a conviction, that it is the wish of Congress to give every encouragement to merit, and that they would cheerfully embrace so favorable an opportunity of manifesting this disposition. I had it in contemplation at the time, in case no other method more eligible could be adopted, to make him an offer of a place in my family. I have consulted the committee of Congress upon the subject, and we were mutually of opinion, that giving Captain Lee the command of two troops of horse on the proposed establishment, with the rank of major, to act as in independent partisan corps, would be a mode of rewarding him very advantageous to the service. Captain Lee's genius particularly adapts him to a command of this nature; and it will be the most agreeable to him of any station in which he could be placed.

I beg leave to recommend this measure to Congress, and shall be obliged by their decision as speedily as may be convenient. The campaign is fast approaching, and there will probably be very little time to raise and prepare the corps for it. It is a part of the plan to give Mr. Lindsey the command of the second troop, and to make Mr. Peyton captain-lieutenant of the first.

I am, with the highest esteem and respect, &c. [20]

---

[20] The above recommendation was confirmed by Congress in all its particulars. In the preamble to the resolve, it is stated, that "Captain Henry Lee, of the Light Dragoons, by the whole tenor of his conduct during the last campaign, has proved himself a brave and prudent officer, rendered essential service to his country, and acquired to himself, and the corps he commanded, distinguished honor."—*Journals, April 7th*

To the President of Congress, English-town, 1 July, 1778

Sir,

I embrace this first moment of leisure to give Congress a more full and particular account of the movements of the army under my command since its passing the Delaware, than the situation of our affairs would heretofore permit. I had the honor to advise them, that, on the appearances of the enemy's intention to march through Jersey becoming, serious. I had detached General Maxwell's brigade, in conjunction with the militia of that State, to interrupt and impede their progress by every obstruction in their power, so as to give time to the army under my command to come up with them, and take advantage of any favorable circumstances that might present themselves. The army, having proceeded to Coryell's Ferry, and crossed the Delaware at that place, I immediately detached Colonel Morgan with a select corps of six hundred men to reinforce General Maxwell, and marched with the main body towards Princeton.

The slow advance of the enemy had greatly the air of design, and led me, with others, to suspect that General Clinton, desirous of a general action, was endeavouring to draw us down into the lower country, in order, by a rapid movement, to gain our right, and take possession of the strong grounds above us. This consideration, and to give the troops time to repose and refresh themselves from the fatigues they had experienced from rainy and excessively hot weather, determined me to halt at Hopewell township about five miles from Princeton, where we remained till the morning of the 25th. On the preceding day I made a second detachment of fifteen hundred chosen troops under Brigadier-

General Scott, to reinforce those already in the vicinity of the enemy, the more effectually to annoy and delay their march. The next day the army moved to Kingston; and, having received intelligence that the enemy were prosecuting their route towards Monmouth Court-House, I despatched a thousand select men under Brigadier-General Wayne, and sent the Marquis de Lafayette to take the command of the whole advanced corps, including Maxwell's brigade and Morgan's light-infantry, with orders to take the first fair opportunity of attacking the enemy's rear.

In the evening of the same day the whole army marched from Kingston, where our baggage was left, with intention to preserve a proper distance for supporting the advanced corps, and arrived at Cranberry early the next morning. The intense heat of the weather, and a heavy storm unluckily coming on, made it impossible to resume our march that day without great inconvenience and injury to the troops. Our advanced corps, being differently circumstanced, moved from the position it had held the night before, and took post in the evening on the Monmouth road about five miles from the enemy's rear, in expectation of attacking them next morning on their march. The main body having remained at Cranberry, the advanced corps was found to be too remote, and too far upon the right, to be supported in case of an attack either upon or from the enemy; which induced me to send orders to the Marquis to file off by his left towards Englishtown, which he accordingly executed early in the morning of the 27th.

The enemy, in marching from Allentown, had changed their disposition, and placed their best troops in the rear, consisting of all the grenadiers, light-infantry, and chasseurs of the line. This alteration made it necessary to increase the number of our advanced corps; in consequence of which I detached Major-General Lee with two brigades to join the Marquis at Englishtown, on whom of course the command of the whole devolved, amounting to about five thousand men. The main body marched the same day, and encamped within three miles of that place. Morgan's corps was left hovering on the enemy's right flank; and the Jersey militia, amounting at this time to about seven or eight hundred men, under General Dickinson, on their left.

The enemy were now encamped in a strong position, with their right extending about a mile and a half beyond the Court-House to the parting of the roads leading to Shrewsbury and Middletown, and their left along the road from Allentown to Monmouth, about three miles on this side of the Court-House. Their right flank lay on the skirt of a small wood, while their left was secured by a very thick one, a morass running towards their rear, and their whole front covered by a wood, and, for a considerable extent towards the left, with a morass. In this situation they halted till the morning of the 28th. Matters being thus situated, and having had the best information, that, if the enemy were once arrived at the Heights of Middletown, ten or twelve miles from where they were, it would be impossible to attempt any thing against them with a prospect of success, I determined to attack their rear the moment they should get in motion from their present ground. I communicated my intention to General Lee, and ordered him to make his disposition for the attack, and to keep his troops constantly lying upon their arms, to be in readiness at the shortest notice. This was done with respect to the troops under my immediate command.

About five in the morning General Dickinson sent an express, informing that the front of the enemy had begun their march. I instantly put the army in motion, and sent orders by one of my aids to General Lee to move on and attack them, unless there should be very powerful reasons to the contrary, acquainting him at the same time, that I was marching to support him, and, for doing it with the greater expedition and convenience, should make the men disencumber themselves o their packs and blankets. After marching about five miles, to my great surprise and mortification, I met the whole advanced corps retreating, and, as I was told, by General Lee's orders, without having made any opposition, except one fire, given by a party under the command of Colonel Butler, on their being charged by the enemy's cavalry, who were repulsed. I proceeded immediately to the rear of the corps, which I found closely pressed by the enemy, and gave directions for forming part of the retreating troops, who, by the brave and spirited conduct of the officers, aided by some pieces of well-served artillery, checked the enemy's advance, and gave time to make a disposition of the left wing and second line of the army upon an eminence, and in a wood a little in the rear, covered by a morass in front. On this were placed some batteries of cannon by Lord Stirling, who commanded the left wing, which played upon the enemy with great effect, and, seconded by parties of infantry detached to oppose them, effectually put a stop to their advance.

General Lee being detached with the advanced corps, the command of the right wing, for the occasion, was given to General Greene. For the expedition of the march, and to counteract any attempt to turn our right, I had ordered him to file off by the new church, two miles from Englishtown, and fall into the Monmouth road, a small distance in the rear or the Court-House, while the rest of the column moved directly on towards the Court-House. On intelligence of the retreat, he marched up and took a very advantageous position on the right. The enemy by this time, finding themselves warmly opposed in front, made an attempt to turn our left flank; but they were bravely repulsed and driven back by detached parties of infantry. They also made a movement to our right with as little success, General Greene having advanced a body of troops with artillery to a commanding piece or ground; which not only disappointed their design of turning our right, but severely enfiladed those in front of the left wing. In addition to this, General Wayne advanced with a body of troops, and kept up so severe and well-directed a fire, that the enemy were soon compelled to retire behind the defile where the first stand in the beginning of the action bad been made.

In this situation the enemy had both their flanks secured by thick woods and morasses, while their front could only be approached through a narrow pass. I resolved nevertheless to attack them; and for that purpose ordered General Poor, with his own and the Carolina brigade, to move round upon their right, and General Woodford upon, their left, and the artillery to gall them in front. But the impediments in their way prevented their getting within reach before it was dark. They remained upon the ground they had been directed to occupy during the night, with the intention to begin the attack early the next morning; and the army continued lying upon their arms in the field of action, to be in readiness to support them. In the mean time the enemy were employed in removing their wounded, and about twelve o'clock at night marched away in such silence, that, though General Poor lay extremely near them, they effected their retreat without his knowledge. They carried off all their wounded, except four officers and about forty privates, whose wounds were too dangerous to permit their removal.

The extreme heat of the weather, the fatigue of the men from their march through a deep sandy country almost entirely destitute of water, and the distance the enemy had gained by marching in the night, made a pursuit impracticable and fruitless. It would have answered no valuable purpose, and would have been fatal to numbers of our men, several of whom died the preceding day with heat.

Were I to conclude my account of this day's transactions, without expressing my obligations to the officers or the army in general, I should do injustice to their merit, and violence to my own feelings. They seemed to vie with each other in manifesting their zeal and bravery. The catalogue of those, who distinguished themselves, is too long to admit of particularizing individuals. I cannot, however, forbear mentioning Brigadier-General Wayne, whose good conduct and bravery through the whole action deserves particular commendation. The behaviour of the troops in general, after they recovered from the first surprise occasioned by the retreat of the advanced corps, was such as could not be surpassed. All the artillery, both officers and men, that were engaged, distinguished themselves in a remarkable manner.

Enclosed. Congress will be pleased to receive a return of our killed, wounded, and missing. Among the first were Lieutenant-Colonel Bunner of Pennsylvania, and Major

Dickinson of Virginia, both officers of distinguished merit, and much to be regretted. The enemy's slain, left on the field, and buried by us, according to the return of the persons assigned to that duty; were four officers and two hundred and forty-five privates. In the former number was the honorable Colonel Monckton. Exclusive of these, they buried some themselves, as there were several new graves near the field of battle. How many men they may have had wounded cannot be determined; but, from the usual proportion, the number must have been considerable. There were a few prisoners taken.

The peculiar situation of General Lee, at this time requires that I should say nothing of his conduct. He is now in arrest. The charges against him, with such sentence as the court-martial may decree in his case, shall be transmitted for the approbation or disapprobation of Congress, as soon as it shall be passed.

Being fully convinced by the gentlemen of this country, that the enemy cannot be hurt or injured in their embarkation at Sandy Hook, the place to which they are going, and unwilling to get too far removed from the North River, I put the troops in motion early this morning, and shall proceed that way, leaving the Jersey brigade, Morgan's corps, and other light parties (the militia being all dismissed) to hover about them, to countenance desertion, and to prevent depredations as far as possible. After they embark, the former will take post in the neighbourhood of Elizabethtown, the latter rejoin the corps from which they were detached.

I have the honor to be, &c.